How to Use Google Classroom & Other Google Apps

A Step By Step Beginner's Guide for Online Teaching

By

SAHEED, Y. K. Ph.D.

Table of Contents

Introduction and Google Drive for files

Google Drive is a free, web-based office suite, data storage service and online storage solution offered by Google. According to Wikipedia, Google Drive is a file storage and synchronization service developed by Google, Launched on April 24, 2012. Google Drive allows users to store files on their servers, synchronize files across devices, and share files. In addition to a website, Google Drive offers apps with offline capabilities for Windows and macOS computers, and Android and iOS smartphones and tablets. Google Drive encompasses Google Docs, Google Sheets, and Google Slides, which are a part of an office suite that permits collaborative editing of documents, spreadsheets, presentations, drawings, forms, and more. Files created and edited through the office suite are saved in Google Drive.

Google Drive offers users 15 gigabytes of free storage through Google One. Google One also offers 100 gigabytes, 200 gigabytes, 2 terabytes, 10 terabytes,

20 terabytes, and 30 terabytes offered through optional paid plans. Files uploaded can be up to 5 terabytes in size. Users can change privacy settings for individual files and folders, including enabling sharing with other users or making content public. On the website, users can search for an image by describing its visuals, and use natural language to find specific files, such as "find my Computer Architecture Lecture note".

Upload Files and Folders to Google Drive

You can upload, view, share, and edit files with Google Drive. When you upload a file to Google Drive, it will take up space in your Drive, even if you upload to a folder owned by someone else.

Types of files

- Documents
- Images
- Audio
- Video

Getting started with Google Drive

If you have a Google account, then you already have access to Google Drive. If you do not have a Google account, you can sign up easily by creating a new account from the accounts.google web page. Consumer accounts are free and business or enterprise accounts may be provided by your employer.

Once you have a Google account, you can upload, store and share your files using Google Drive by means of three different methods:

- Google Drive online
- Google Drive computer application
- Google Drive mobile application

While Apple's iCloud and Microsoft's OneDrive offer similar features and apps, Google Drive is the only cloud storage service that rivals DropBox by spanning out into less popular OS platforms. Google Drive is heavily integrated into ChromeOS (Chromebook),as well as available for many other Linux desktop distributions.

How to use Google Drive online

To use Google Drive from any modern web browser, simply open the browser of your choice. Navigate to drive.google.com. If you are not already signed into Google, you will be asked to enter your Google account credentials to sign in.

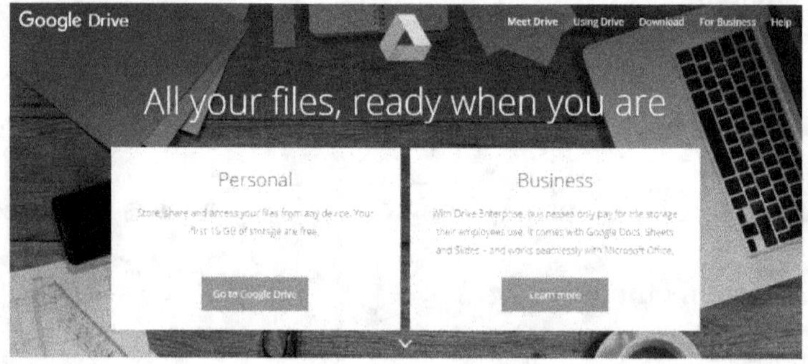

google drive interface

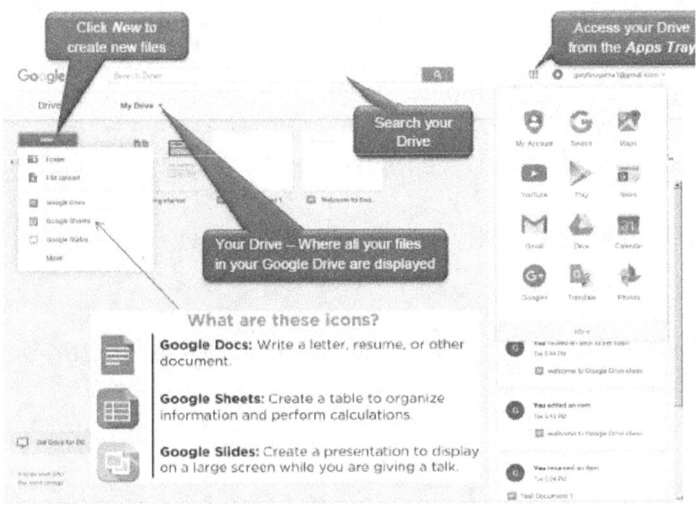

Google drive home page

Basic Terms

Apps Tray: Shows all of the features included with your Gmail account. The icon looks like this:

Upload: Copy a document or file from your computer or flash drive to the Internet.

Download: Copy a document from the Internet to your computer or flash drive.

Share: Allow other users to see (and potentially edit) files you have in your Google Drive.

Sync: Short for "synchronization," this is when Google Drive duplicates files on your device in "The Cloud."

The Cloud: Many people get confused by this term, but it simply means *online storage*.

Google Drive menu

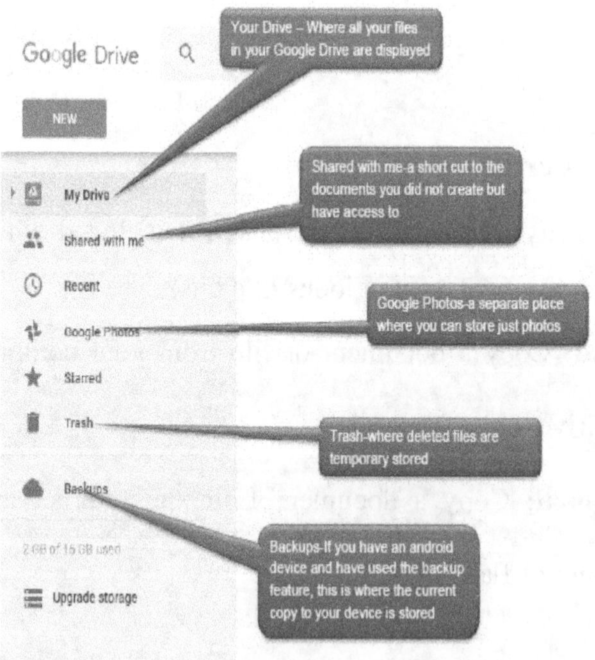

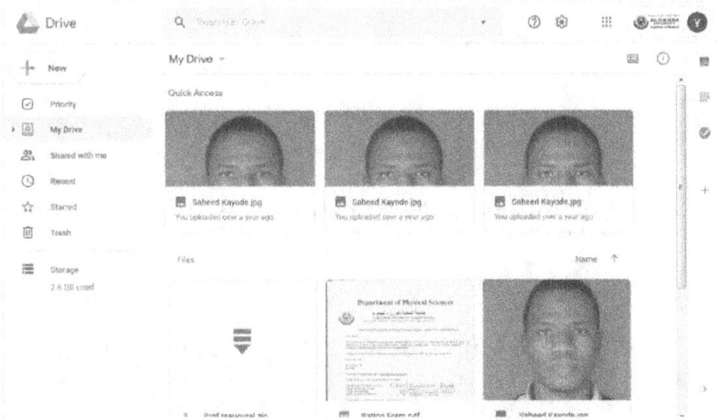

The google drive homepage has a simple user interface

The Google Drive homepage has a simple user interface (UI). The Dashboard along the top of the browser window allows you to adjust settings, perform Google Drive content searches, and manage or share files. To use the dashboard:

- Click or tap the Search box and enter in keywords to perform a search of your Google Drive content.

- Click or tap the Google Apps icon to access other Google services, like Gmail or YouTube.

- Click or tap the Notifications icon to view account notifications.

- Click or tap the Google Account icon to sign in and out of your account.

- Click or tap the New button to create a new file with one of the connected apps, create new folders, and upload files and folders to your cloud.

- Click or tap the link icon to get a shareable link to your file which allows you to grant access to others.

- Click or tap the share icon to send a shareable copy of your file directly via email.

- Click or tap the remove icon to move a file or folder from your cloud to the trash.

- Click or tap the more actions icon for more file management options (folder colors, open files with connected apps, file/folder sorting, and file/folder downloads).

- Click or tap the View/Layout icon to change the file and folder arrangement from list view to grid view.

- Click or tap the View Details icon to view file details such as size, type, previews, and shared status.

- Click or tap the Settings icon for Google Drive settings.

Along the left hand side of the browser window is a sidebar that organizes the content and features in an easy-to-digest layout. To use the sidebar:

- Click or tap My Drive to view and manage the files stored on your cloud.

- Click or tap Computers to view and manage all the computers and mobile devices synced to your Google Drive account.

- Click or tap Shared with me to view and manage other's files stored on other Google Drive accounts that have been shared with you.

- Click or tap Recent to view all recent Google Drive activity.

- Click or tap Google Photos to view and manage your photo storage.

- Click or tap Starred to view all of your favorite or important files.

- Click or tap Trash to view or empty items you placed in the trash for removal.

- Click or tap Backups to view and manage backups of device and app data.

- Click or tap Upgrade Storage to be routed to a web page containing larger tier storage price plans.

Navigating a Document

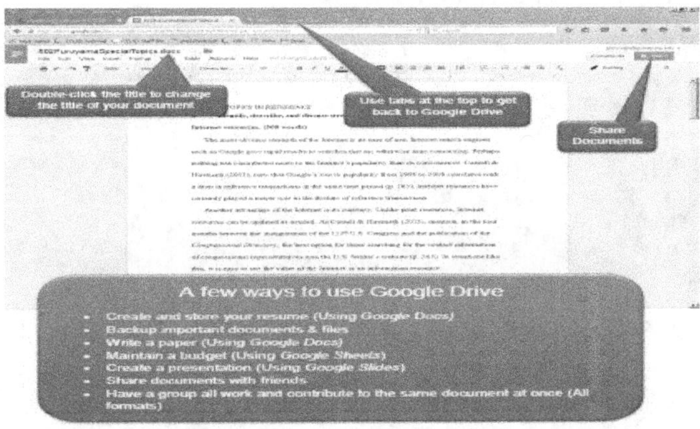

Uploading a File Using Google Drive

Uploading files to the Internet simply means you are saving a copy of a file on the Internet. Uploading files to Google Drive allows you to access your files from any computer with an Internet connection!

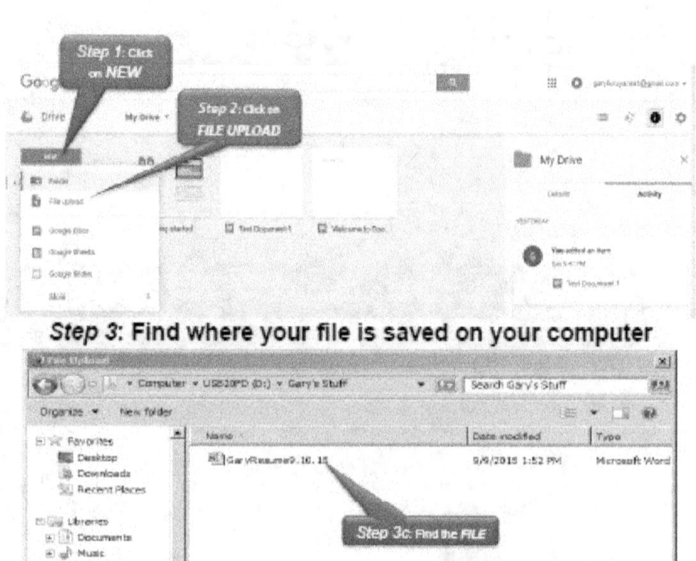

Step 3: Find where your file is saved on your computer

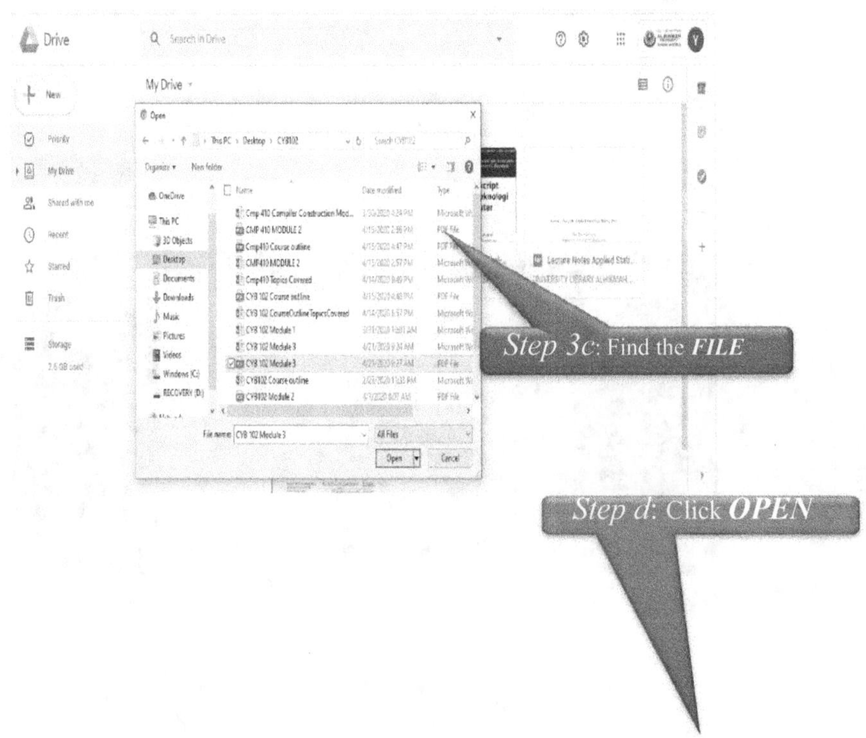

Downloading Files

Downloading saves a copy of a file from your Google Drive to your computer. Once it is saved to your computer, you can upload or change a file as needed.

Open with Google Docs
MODULE 2
STRUCTURE OF THE COMPILER DESIGN
Phases of a compiler: A compiler operates in phases. A phase is a logically interrelated operation that takes source program in one representation and produces output in another representation. The phases of a compiler are shown in below
There are two phases of compilation.
a. Analysis (Machine Independent/Language Dependent)
b. Synthesis (Machine Dependent/Language independent)
Compilation process is partitioned into no-of-sub processes called 'phases'.
Lexical Analysis:-
LA or Scanners reads the source program one character at a time, carving the source program into a sequence of atomic units called tokens
source program

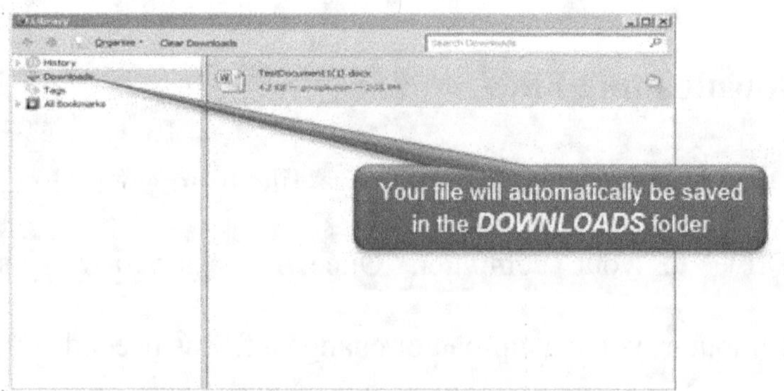

History
Downloads
Tags
All Bookmarks
Organize
Clear Downloads
Search Downloads
TestDocument1(1).docx
Your file will automatically be saved in the DOWNLOADS folder

Google Classroom

Google Classroom is a free web service, developed

by Google for schools, that aims to simplify creating,

distributing, and grading assignments in a paperless way.

The primary purpose of Google Classroom is to streamline

the process of sharing files between teachers and students.

Google Classroom combines Google Drive for assignment

creation and distribution, Google

Docs, Sheets and Slides for writing, Gmail for

communication, and Google Calendar for scheduling.

Students can be invited to join a class through a private

code, or automatically imported from a school domain.

Each class creates a separate folder in the respective user's

Drive, where the student can submit work to be graded by a

teacher. Mobile apps, available

for iOS and Android devices, let users take photos and attach to assignments, share files from other apps, and access information offline. Teachers can monitor the progress for each student, and after being graded, teachers can return work along with comments.

Steps to Create Lecture Period using Google Classroom

1. Go to www.google.com and sign in with your google account.

2. Click the google apps symbol at the top right and click again to look for Classroom. Alternatively, if it is not available there, visit classroom.google.com.

Click the button in the middle of the page.

4. Create a Google Account by clicking on the link.

5. On the right side of the page, **fill in the necessary information to create your Google**

Account. You will have to choose your own username and password. (**It is recommended to write this information down elsewhere, so that you don't forget it**).

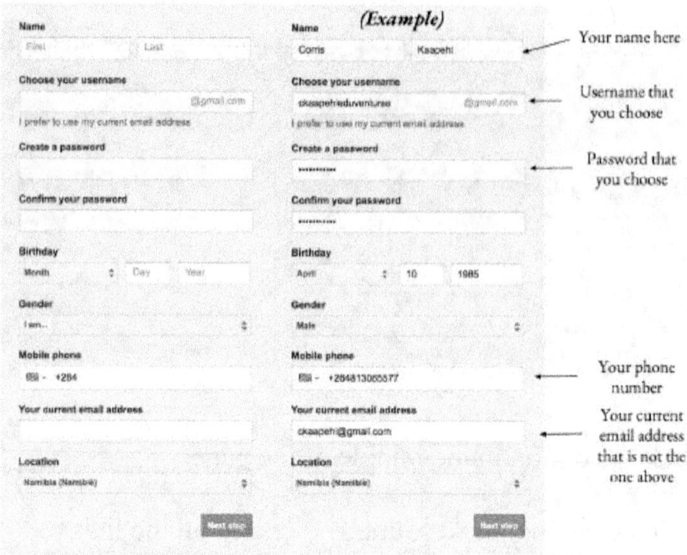

6. After you have filled out all of the necessary information, click the **Next step** button.

7. Click the **Continue to Classroom** button in the middle of the page.

You have now successfully created a Google Classroom account!

Change Your Profile Photo

1. At the top left, click Menu.

2. Scroll down and click **Settings.**

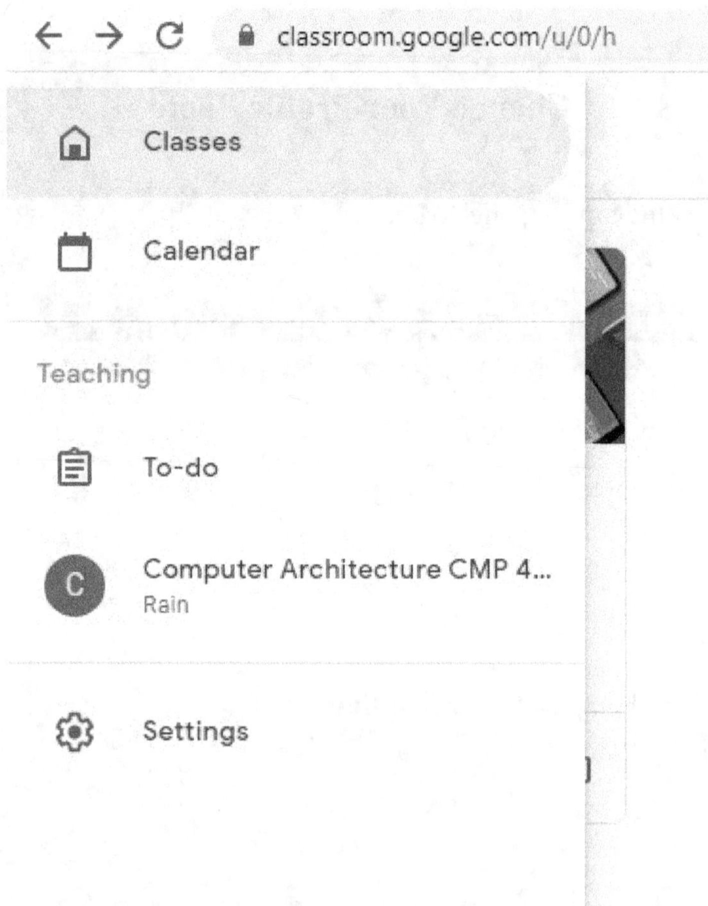

3. Under **Profile picture.** click **Change.**

4. Click or drag a photo from your computer.

5. **(Optional)** Resize the box over your photo.

6. Click **Set as profile photo.**

Customize your Notifications

1. At the top left, click Menu ☰ .

2. Click **Settings** in the bottom left (you might need to scroll down).

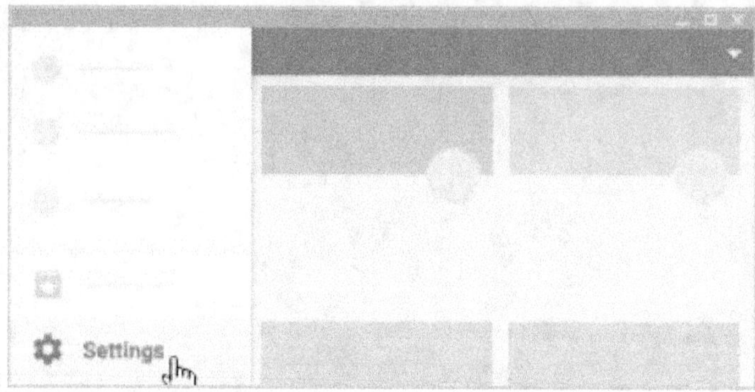

3. Click any notification to turn it on or off.

4. **(Optional)** To turn all notifications off, at **Receive email notifications**, click Turn off.

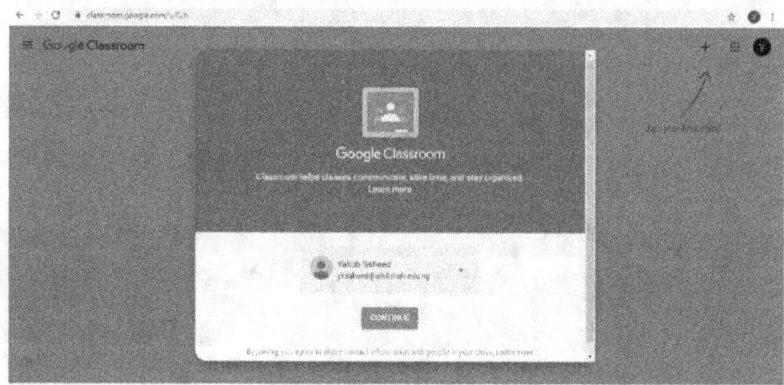

How to Create a Class with Google Classroom

Creating classes is the first step for teachers who want to set up an online space with Google classroom. Here's how.

1. Navigate to https://classroom.google.com

2. Log in and pick your role as a teacher.

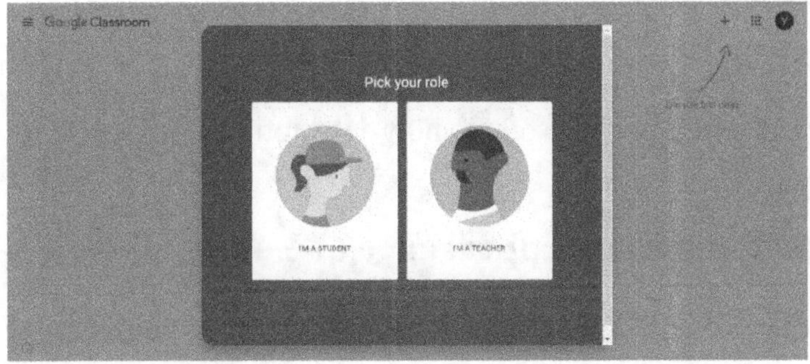

3. Click the "+" sign in the top right-hand corner next to your Google account

4. Select "Create Class", then give it a name and a section, and click "Create"

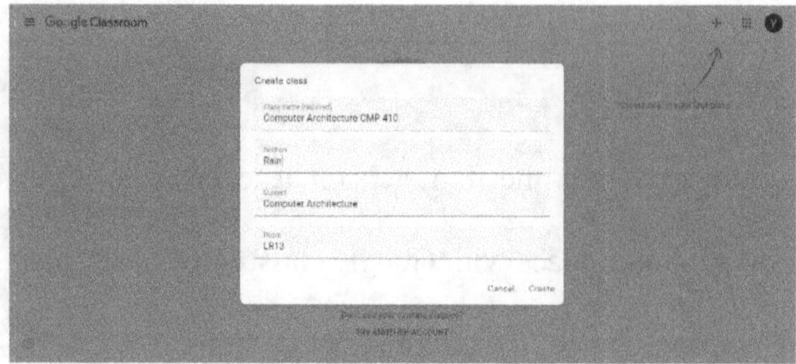

The "Section" field is a secondary descriptor for your class, so here you may want to add something like 1st period, a grade level, or some other short description.

Customize the Appearance of Your Class

When you create your class for the first time, you are given a default header image. This is the image that students will see when they click on your class to access assignments and announcements.

You can customize this image with a few quick steps.

1. In the lower right corner of the image, you will find "Change Class Theme"

2. Click "Change Class Theme" to open a gallery of photos you can choose for your class.

3. Choose a photo from the gallery, then click "Pick Class Theme" to change your header image.

There are a variety of images to choose from, but most are themed on some kind of academic subject. For instance, you could choose books for Language Arts classes, a piano for Music, colored pencils for Art, and so forth.

Check out the gallery of images you can use to customize your class

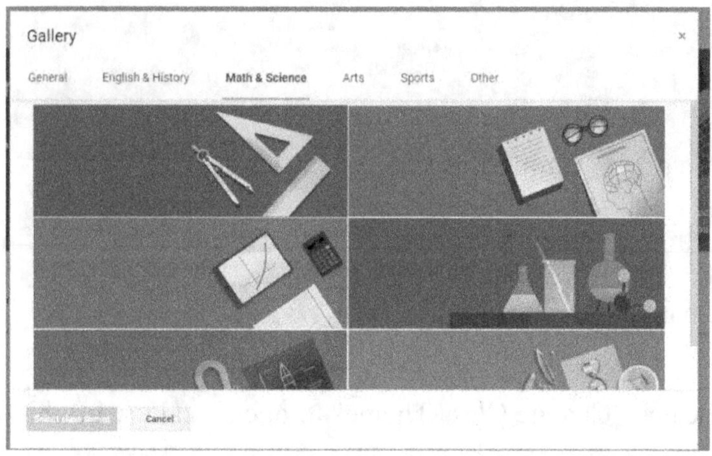

Google Classroom consists of three (3) main sections;

1. The stream: This is a place where we can communicate with people. Stream allow us to communicate with our class, the teacher can post announcements, and, respond to students posts.

Students posts and comments can be seen in the Stream section

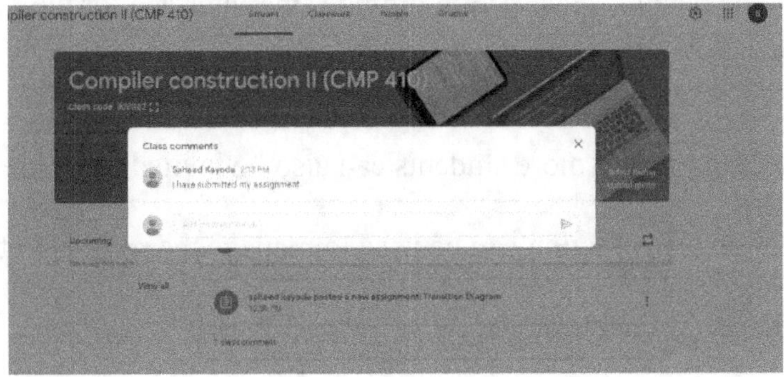

2. The Classwork: This section is the heart of using google classroom. In the Classwork page, we can create assignment and questions, use topics to

organize classwork into modules or units and order

work the way you want students to see it.

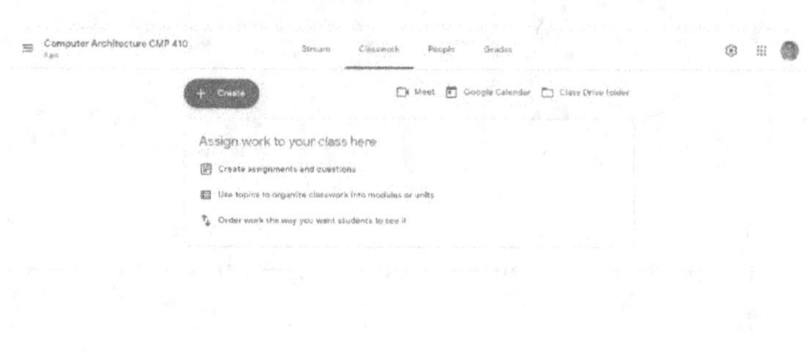

3. The people: This section provides the interface for the

teachers and students. Co-teachers can be invited through

this section and more students can also be invited via this

section. This section can be used to manage the people that

are part of the class.

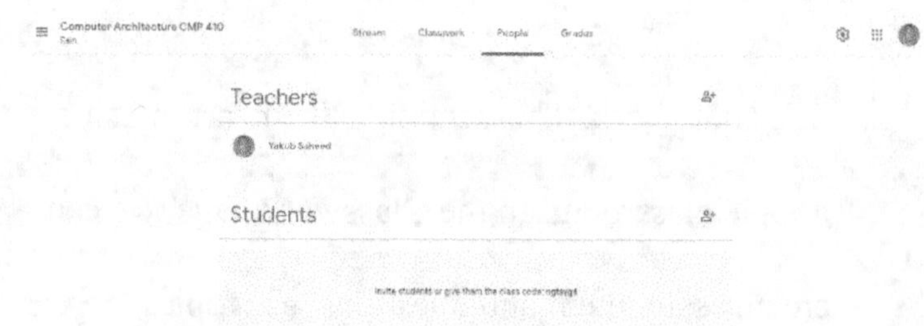

Steps to Join Lecture by Students

Add students via email invitation

1. Click the **STUDENTS** button in the top middle of the page.

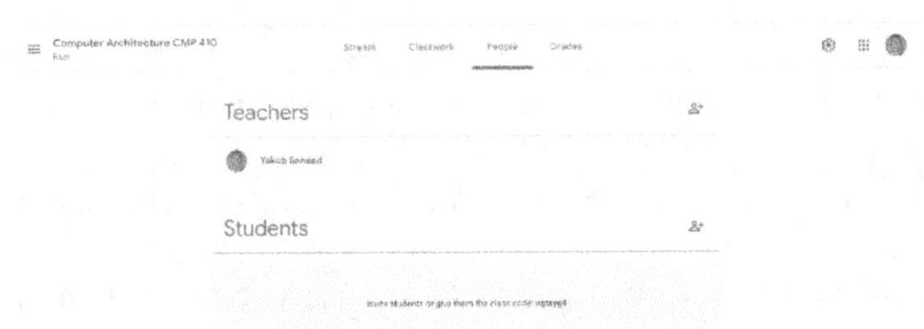

2. Click the **INVITE STUDENTS** button at the top of the page.

3. Click on where it says

Type a name or email

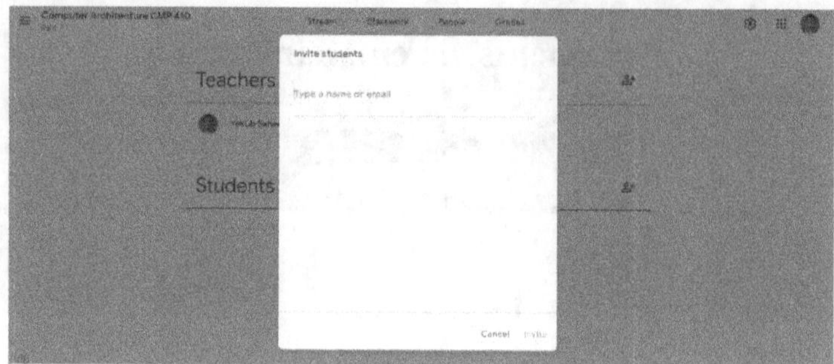

4. Enter in the email of the students that you would like to invite. If you have emailed them before, you can simply type their name in the box and their email will pop up below where you are typing. You can invite more than one student at once.

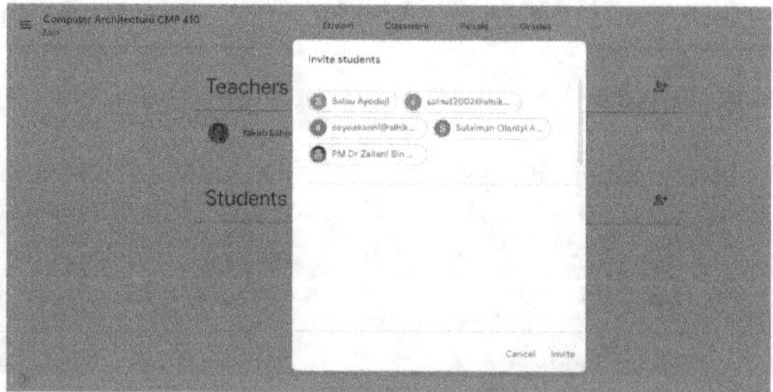

5. Once you have entered in all of the students that you would like to invite, click on the **INVITE** button. An email will be sent to them inviting them to be a student in your class.

Add students via class code

1. In the **STUDENTS** page of your class, on the left will be the class code.

2. Ask the students to join your class using this code, which is different for every class.

Invite students or give them the class code: ngtsyg4

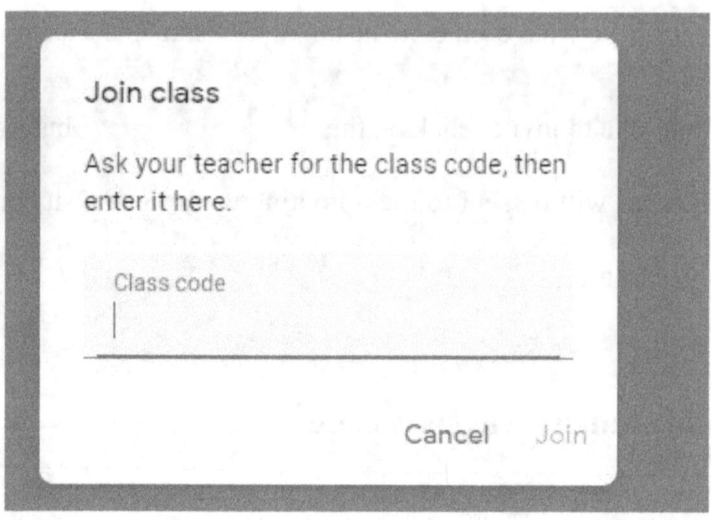

How to Add Students in Classroom

There are two ways to add students to your class, 1) Is by using the class code.

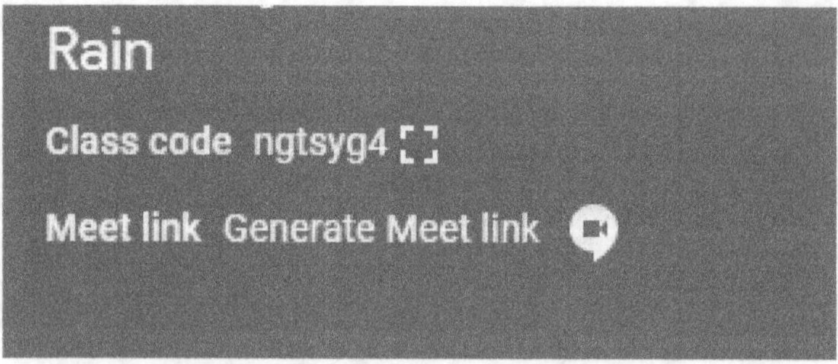

When the students are to join the class, the students

navigate to Join class and input the class code or preferably

the teacher invite them via Email.

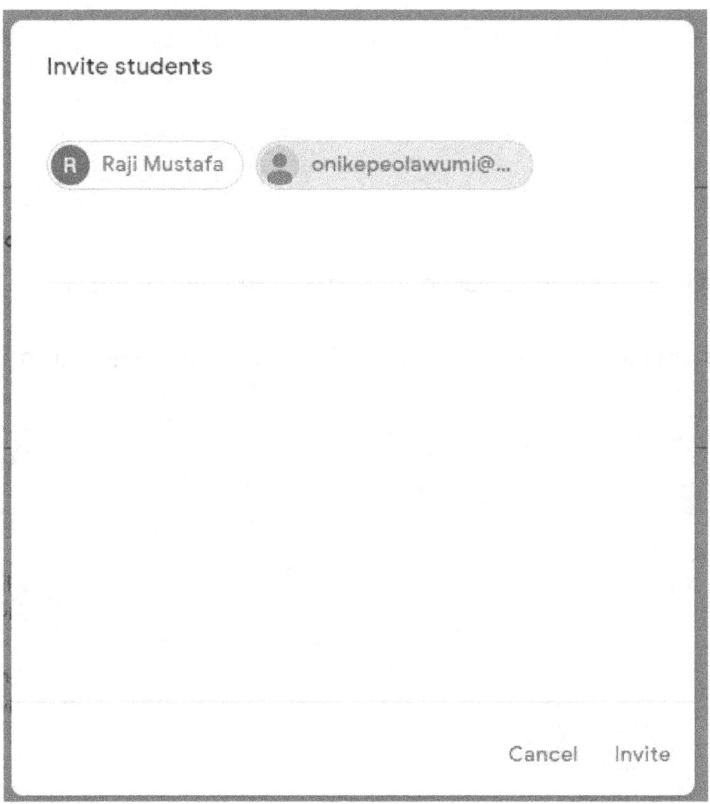

After, the invitation is sent to the students, invited would

show in the panel page.

When the students accept the invitation, the invited would disappear and the students would be listed as a student in the class.

Steps to Start New Lecture by Teachers

Adding Teachers

1. Navigate to TEACHER button in the top middle of the page, and, click this  symbol.

Teachers

Yakub Saheed

2. Click the Invite teachers button at the top of the page.

3. Click on where it says.

Type a name or email

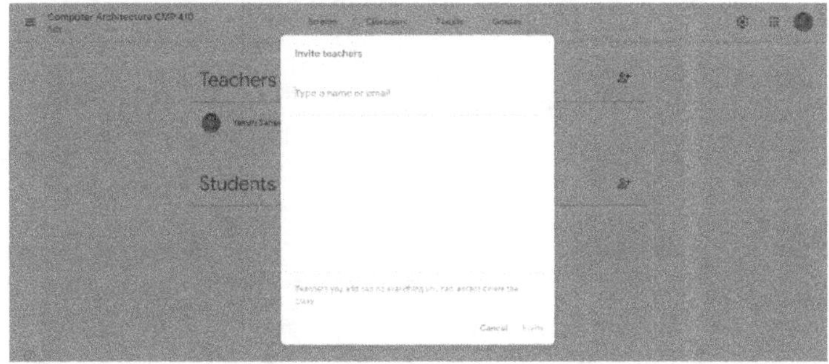

4. Enter in the email of the teachers that you would like to invite. If you have emailed them before, you can simply type their name in the box and their email will pop up

below where you are typing. You can invite more than one

teacher at once.

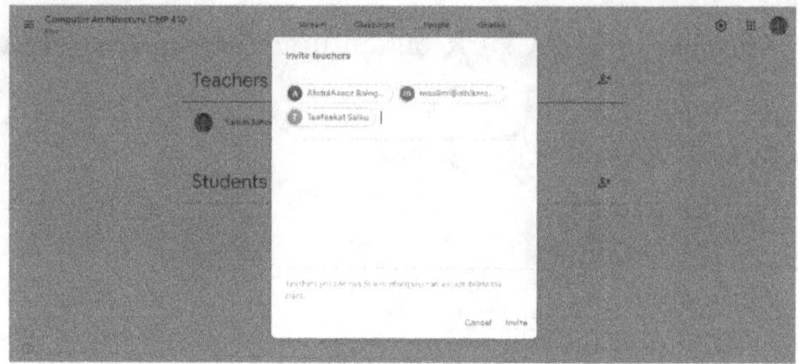

5. Once you have entered in all of the teachers that you

would like to invite, click on the **INVITE** button.

An email will be sent to them inviting them to be a teacher

in your class.

How to Control Activities on Google Classroom

View Your Class Resource Page

1. Click Classwork.

2. Here you can click on a variety of options to open them.

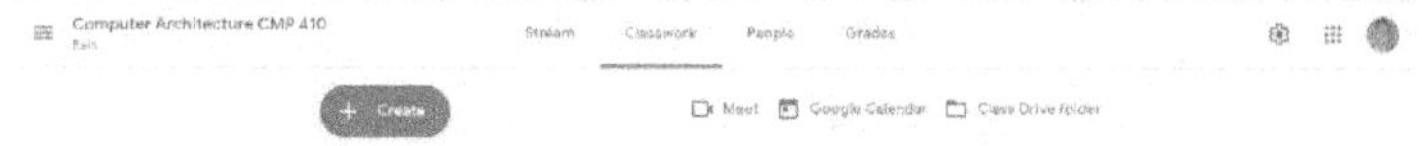

Meet video meetings

Google meet can connect you with students for distance learning.

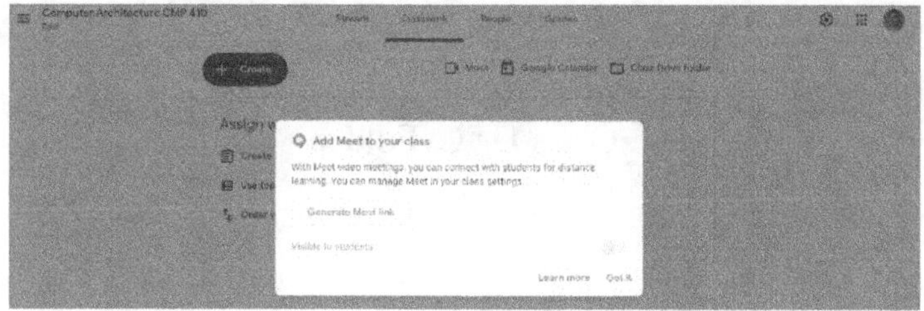

How to use Google Calendar

Google Calendar: The google calendar allows you to add events to the course calendar. It automatically creates the course calendar for the teacher, events can be added for students to see what is coming up.

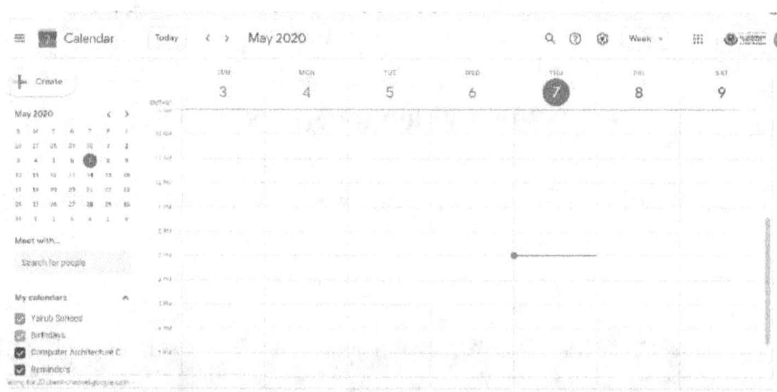

Class Drive Folder

1. Click on Classwork.

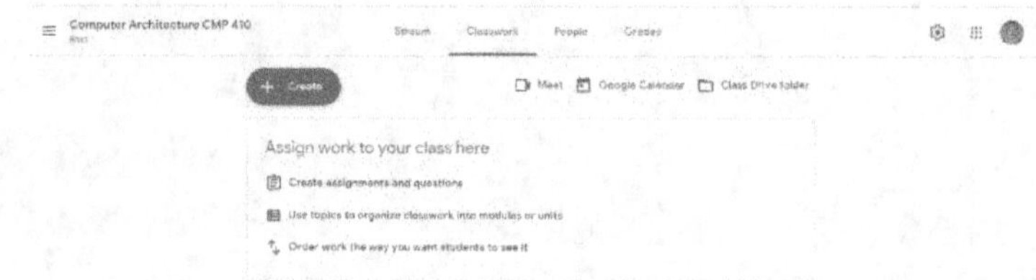

2. At the top right, click Class Drive folder button.

- The **Class Drive Folder** can only be view by the administrators

- When students open the **Class Drive Folder** they will only see the files that have been shared with them (i.e. Files that have been put in the class through an announcement, assignment or question)

4. Right click on a file that has been shared with the class and click **Share** button

5. The following page will pop-up:

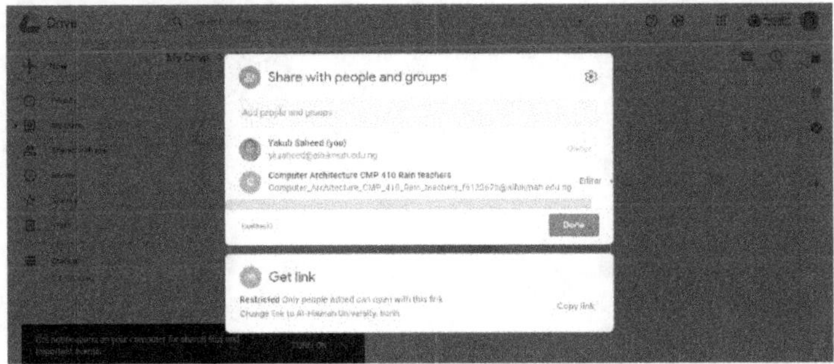

Announcement

Post an Announcement

1. If you are not already on the Stream page, click on the button

Stream

2. Your screen may say "Stream was updated" in the top middle. If it does, click on the button.

3. Navigate to Share something with your class and click on it.

4. Click to communicate with your class.

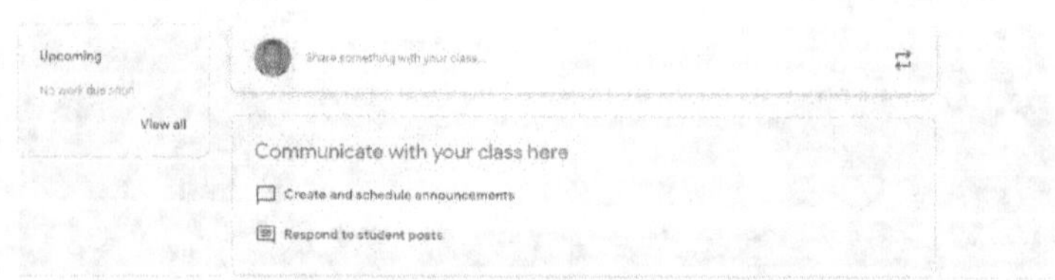

The information to be announced and share with the class can be input in the dialog box as below. This can be done for each student or preferably all students at once.

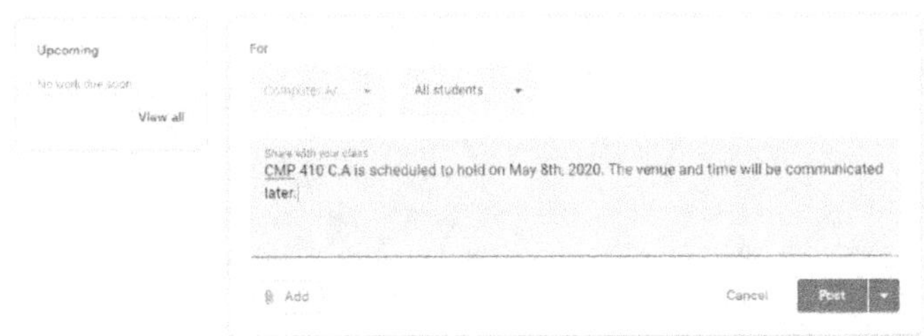

Files can also be attached for the students, the files can be from Google Drive, link, file or You tube.

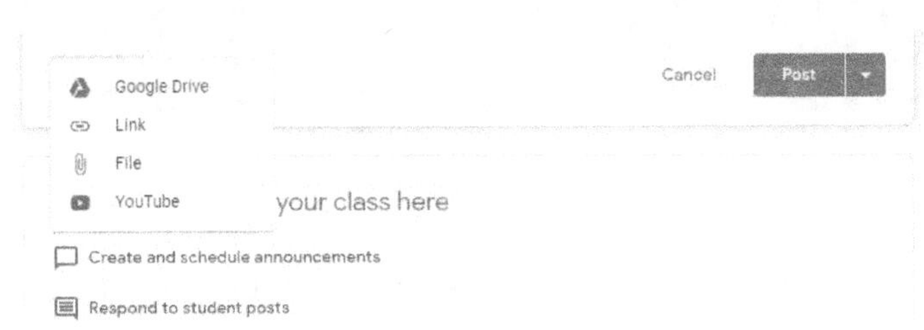

Add a Topic

1. Go to Classwork and hit **+ Create** button.

2. On the left-hand side of your "Classwork" page, you will see list of drop down menus, click Topic.

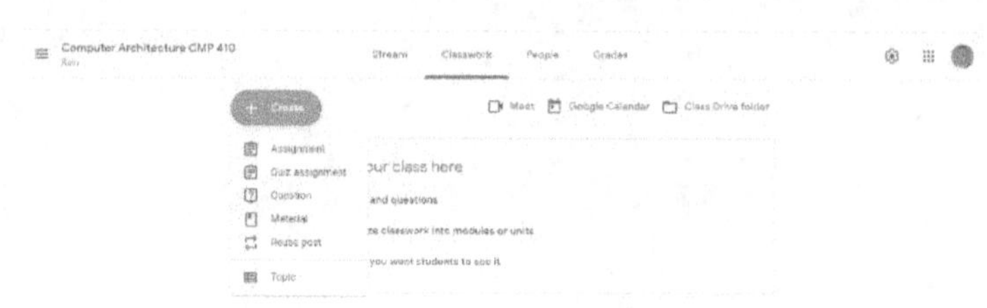

3. The Add topic dialog appear, then add topic.

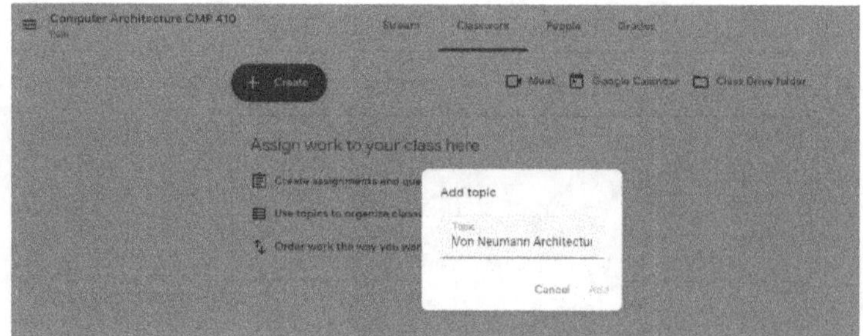

The list of topics in Google classroom can be listed to be more than one, for students to see all the topics covered in a course.

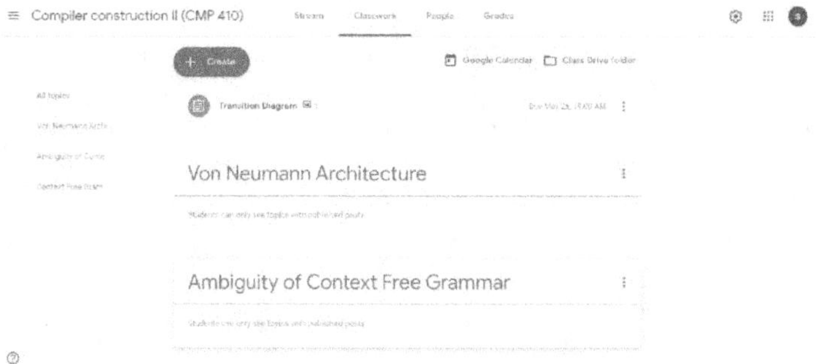

The topics can have the rename, Delete, copy link and move down operations. These operations can be performed to suit the choice of the teacher.

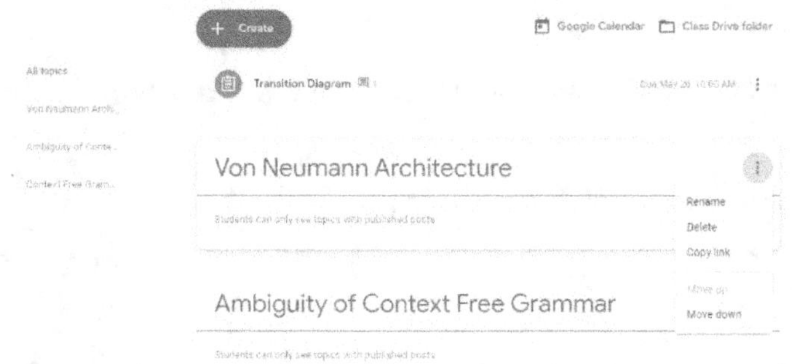

Originality Report

The originality report is another great feature in the Assignment Interface located in the lower part of the right hand.

The originality report can be used to test the similarity index and the originality of the assignment submitted by the students. The originality reports can be done on three assignments per class.

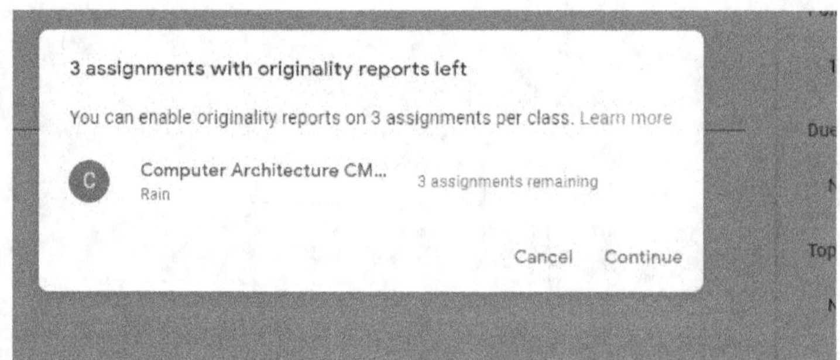

How to Add Materials

Step 1: Go to Classwork and click on Create button.

Step 2. Click on the material option to insert the title and the description of the material.

Step 3. The materials can be added from Google Drive, Link, file or YouTube and post to all the students or selected students

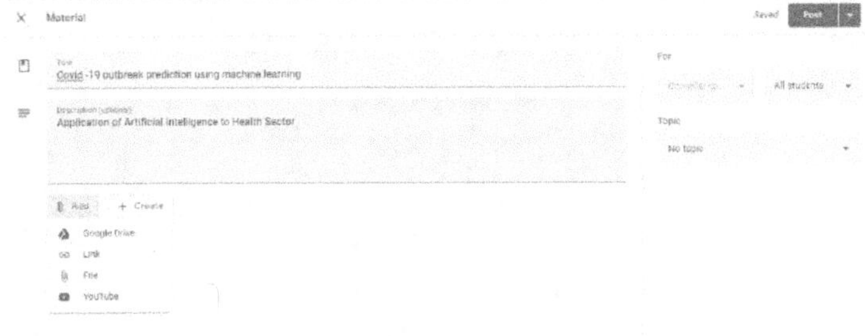

Create Assignments

Create an Assignment in Google Classroom (Part 1)

Assignments can be created, and assigned to students, from inside Google Classroom, and there are number of useful options here for educators. Here's how to add your first assignment.

1. Click on the Classwork and hit the  button.

2. Now click "Assignment" in the drop-down menu.

3. Give your assignment a title and add any additional instructions or a description in the box below

4. After inputting the title and the instructions, the due date can be given.

5. Choose the type of assignment you wish to create by clicking on one of the icons next to the word Assign. Your choices are to upload a file from your computer, attach a file from Google Drive, add a YouTube video, or add a link to a website.

6. Click "Assign" to give this assignment to your students.

If you want to give the assignment to more than one class, click the name of the class at the bottom of the assignment window and choose the classes you want to assign it to.

7. Click the date to choose a due date for your assignment, and, add a time if you want to specify when it due on a given day.

Create an Assignment in Google Classroom (Part 2)

Many teachers who use Google Classroom will likely elect to add an assignment from their Drive, because this is likely where a lot of the teacher's resources are now stored. However, there is an added benefit to choosing a Drive resource in Google Classroom, and that becomes clear with the options you get when you select a file from Drive.

1. Students can view file: Select this option if you want all students to be able to view the file, but not be able to modify it any way. This is ideal for study guides and generic handouts that the whole class need access to.

2. Students can edit file: Choose this if you want all students to be able to edit and work on the same document. This would be ideal for a collaborative class project where students may be working on separate slides in the same Google Presentation, or where they are collaboratively brainstorming ideas for something you want to discuss in your next class.

3. Make a copy for each student: If you pick this option, Classroom will make a copy of the original file for each student in your class and give them editing rights to that file. The teacher's master remains intact and the students have no access to the original file. Choose this is you want to quickly disseminate a paper that has an essay question for students to work on, or a digital worksheet template where students fill in the blanks with their own answers.

This level of automation was possible before Google Classroom, but it is infinitely easier to manage when integrated into this new platform.

Marking Control and Grading

How do the students know that I have graded their assignment? Do I have to grade an assignment out of 100? These questions, and more, are answered below.

- ➢ When the teacher returns an assignment to a student, the teacher no longer has editing rights on that document.

- You can return an assignment to a student without grading it by simply checking the box next to the student's name and clicking Return. This could be useful for assignments submitted in error.

- When you return an assignment to the student, they will automatically receive an email notification informing them of your actions.

- You can change a grade at any time by clicking on the grade and then clicking "Update".

- Clicking the folder button will open the Google Drive folder where all student submissions are stored. This is useful for reviewing all the submitted assignments at one time.

Steps on How to Grade with the Classroom

Step 1: Click on the Grade.

Step 2: Navigate to the student name and click on the

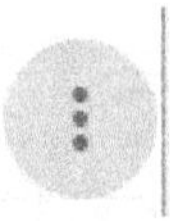

button to show the return and view submission

options.

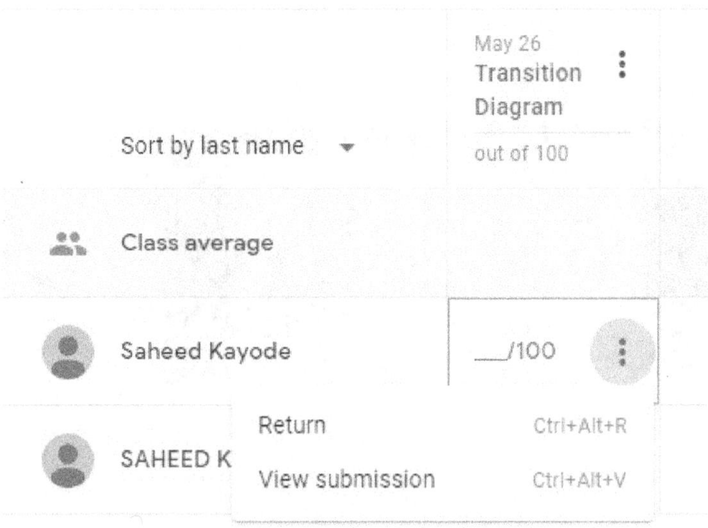

Step 3: Click on the view submission

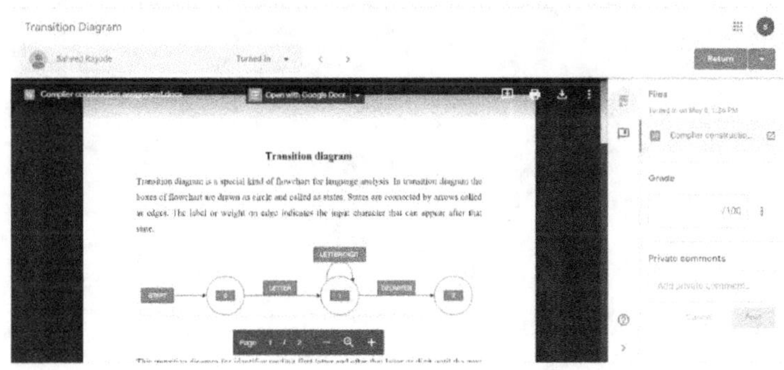

Step 4: The grade score can be input on the left-side panel

of the view option page. Additionally, private comments

can be added like "Excellent performance" in the private comments box.

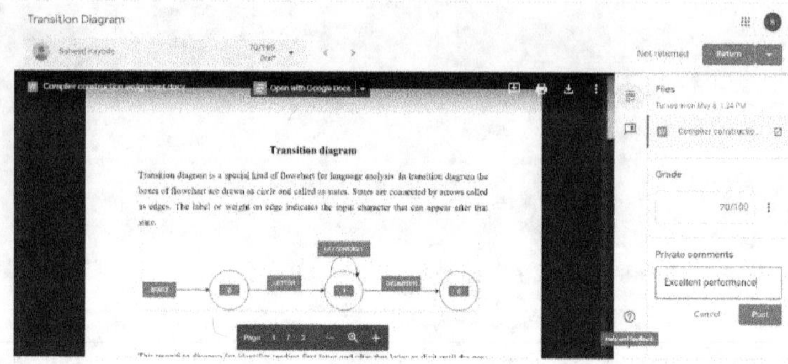

Advantages of Google Classroom

1. **Easy to use and accessible from all devices.**

   Even if you are not a Google user, using Google Classroom is a piece of cake. Apart from being delivered through the Chrome browser, which makes it accessible from all computers, mobile phones, and tablets, it makes it really easy for you to add as many learners as you like, create Google documents to manage assignments and announcements, post YouTube videos, add links, or attach files from Google Drive. Learners will find it equally easy to log in, as well as receive and turn in assignments.

2. **Effective communication and sharing.**

   One of the greatest advantages of Google Classroom is Google Docs; these documents are saved online and shared with a limitless number of people, so when you create an announcement or assignment using a Google doc, your learners can access it immediately through their Google Drive, as long as you have shared it with them. Furthermore, Google Docs are easily organized and personalized in Google Drive folders. In other words, you no longer need emails to share information; you just create a document, share it with as many learners as you want, and voila!

3. **Speeds up the assignment process.**

    How about creating an assignment and distributing it with just a click of a button? And how about learners turning in the completed assignment in a matter of seconds? Assignment process has never been quicker and more effective, as in Google Classroom you can easily check who has submitted their assignment and who is still working on it, as well as offer your feedback immediately.

4. **Effective feedback.**

Speaking of feedback, Google Classroom gives you the opportunity to offer your online support to your learners right away; this means that feedback becomes more effective, as fresh comments and remarks have bigger impact on learners' minds.

5. **No need for paper.**

There might be a day that grading papers would be impossible to imagine; Google Classroom is certainly interested in getting there as soon as possible. By centralizing eLearning materials in one cloud-based location, you have the ability to go paperless and stop worrying about printing, handing out, or even losing your learners' work!

6. **Clean and user-friendly interface.**

Staying loyal to clean Google layout standards, Google Classroom invites you to an environment where every single design detail is simple, intuitive, and user-friendly. Needless to say that, Google

users will feel right at home.

7. **Great commenting system.**

   Learners can comment on specific locations within

   pictures for a variety of online courses.

   Furthermore, you can create URLs for interesting

   comments and using them for further online

   discussion.

8. **Is for everyone.**

   Educators can also join Google Classroom as

   learners, which means that you can create a Google

   Classroom for you and your colleagues and use it

   for faculty meetings, information sharing,

   or professional development.

Limitation

1. **Difficult account management.**

   Google Classroom doesn't allow access from multiple domains. Furthermore, you cannot log in with your personal Gmail to enter it; you need to be logged in Google Apps for Education. As a result, if you have already a personal Google ID, it may be frustrating to juggle multiple Google accounts. For example, if you have a Google document or a photo in your Gmail and you want to share it in the Google Classroom, you will need to save it separately in your computer's hard drive, log out, and then log in again with your Google Classroom account. Quite a hassle.

2. **Limited integration options.**

   Google Classroom hasn't yet integrated with Google Calendar, or any calendar whatsoever, which may cause some problems with organizing

material and assignment deadlines.

3. **Too "googlish".**

First time Google users may get confused, as there

are several buttons with icons familiar only to

Google users. Additionally, despite enhanced

integration between Google and YouTube, which

significantly helps video sharing, support for other

popular tools is not built in, and you may find it

frustrating that you will need to, for example,

convert a simple Word document to a Google Doc

to works with. All in all, you will only find yourself

comfortable in the Google Classroom environment

as long as the tools you are using are aligned with

Google services.

4. **No automated updates.**

Activity feed doesn't update automatically, so

learners will need to refresh regularly in order not to miss important announcements.

5. **Difficult learner sharing.**

Learners cannot share their work with their peers, unless they become "owners" of a document, and even then, they will need to approve sharing options, which will create a chaos if they want to share a document with their, say, 50+ classmates.

6. **Editing problems.**

When you create an assignment and you distribute it to learners, learners become "owners" of the document and they are allowed to edit it. That means that they can delete any part of the assignment they want, which could cause problems, even if it happens accidentally.

7. **No automated quizzes and tests.**

   One of the main reasons that Google Classroom cannot yet fully replace your Learning Management System is that it doesn't provide automated quizzes and tests for your learners. In general, Google Classroom is more suitable for a blended learning experience than a fully online program.

8. **Impersonal.**

   Speaking of a blended learning environment, Google Classroom has not integrated Google Hangouts, which creates a problem; online interaction between teachers and learners is only possible through Google documents. Effective education requires interaction and building relationships with learners, and online discussions are the best way to achieve this in a virtual environment. Unfortunately, there is no way to have a live chat in Google Classroom; at

least, again, not yet.

How to Get Further Help

Dear reader, I hope you find this book very helpful in learning how to how to use Google Classroom. You may find some of the concepts I covered in this book confusing at first.

However, with time and a little more effort, you should be able to use Google Classroom effectively and effortlessly.

I am available for further help. Contact me through my support email below if you need further help, or if you have questions or requests.

Regards,

kayodesaheed@gmail.com

SAHEED Y. K. Ph.D.